UNGRATEFUL

UNGRATEFUL

THE RISE AND FALL OF LABOR UNIONS

JERRY W. WILLIAMS SR.

To order additional copies of this book, contact:
Xlibris Corporation
1-888-795-4274
www.Xlibris.com
Orders@Xlibris.com
116553

CONTENTS

Dedicated to Union Members Everywhere

With special thanks to:

Ronald Roach, for his brilliant research and contribution to this project; my lovely wife, Ruth, who through all the years of our marriage has been a source of strength and help to me as I struggled to fight for the rights of union members and the middle class; and my children, who help keep it all together.

Much has been written about unions, but this book does not go into that pile. I hope it has the impact to inspire. I speak to union members about these matters and find that limited knowledge is abounds. If I can expand one horizon or open one pair of eyes to the importance of having a strong union, then I have succeeded in my goal.

Jerry W. Williams Sr.

Chapter 1

WHAT HAPPENED TO LABOR UNIONS IN THE UNITED STATES? WHY ARE THEY SO WEAK? WHY ARE UNIONS DWINDLING INTO OBSCURITY? AFTER ALL, UNIONS ARE WHAT MADE AMERICA STRONG.

Labor unions afforded many Americans the opportunity to lift themselves up from poverty and live the American dream as middle-class citizens.

Unions in America have correctly been described as a stabilizing force in the national economy. The gains that unions have been able to achieve have brought benefits, direct and indirect, to the public as a whole.

It was labor unions, for example, that spearheaded the drive for public education for every child.

It was labor unions that gave us the five-day workweek, vacations, health benefits, pensions, relaxed work rules, livable wages, and many other pleasures that we now enjoy through hard-fought union negotiations.

So when you hear me talk about the failure of unions, you must understand that it is not so much the union itself that is a failure. In most cases it is the union leaders that members choose to represent them and constant attacks from corporate America on unions and the working class that causes the demise.

The changing conditions of the 1980s and 1990s undermined the position of organized labor, which now represented a shrinking share of the workforce. While more than one-third of employed people belonged to unions in 1945, union membership fell to 24.1 percent of the U.S. workforce in 1979 and to 13.9 percent in 1998.

Dues increases, continuing union contributions to political campaigns, and union members' diligent voter-turnout efforts kept unions' political power from ebbing as much as their membership.

But court decisions and National Labor Relations Board rulings allowing workers to withhold the portion of their union dues used to back, or oppose, political candidates undercut unions' influence.

As if these difficulties were not enough, years of negative publicity about corruption in the big Teamsters Union and other unions have hurt the labor movement. Even unions' past successes in boosting *wages* and benefits and improving the work environment have worked against further gains by making newer, younger workers conclude they no longer need unions to press their causes.

Union arguments that they give workers a voice in almost all aspects of their jobs, including work-site safety and work grievances, are often ignored. The kind of independent-minded young workers who sparked the dramatic rise of high-technology computer firms have little interest in belonging to organizations that they believe quash independence.

I was a guest panelist at a national forum for school teachers in Iowa when a young teacher stood up and made a statement to the audience that in her opinion, union contracts are in the way because the contract doesn't allow her to do the extra things she would like to do as a teacher.

I got an opportunity to ask the teacher a few questions. I asked her if she was satisfied with her pay. She said yes. I asked if she was satisfied with her pension. She answered yes. I asked if she was satisfied with her health care, days off, vacations, working conditions, etc.; she said yes.

I then asked her if she knew that these things were negotiated for her by her union and without the union's presence, all these things can and probably would be taken away and that she would have no recourse of stopping these actions. The young teacher was totally taken aback, and she took her seat.

The majority of union members today takes for granted that union workers fought and, in some cases, died in order to attain decent wages and benefits for the member and his/her family.

Union members in many cases don't understand that the wages, holidays, benefits, pensions, vacations, etc., that they enjoy today were not given to them by the company, but negotiated by their union.

Much of this naivety is a result of union members not knowing the history of the labor movement.

Unions are finding it hard to recruit new members. Perhaps the biggest reason unions face trouble recruiting new members is that in the late 1990s, there was a surprising strength in the economy. In October and November 1999, the *unemployment* rate had fallen to 4.1 percent.

Economists said only people who were between jobs or chronically unemployed were out of work. For all the uncertainties economic changes had produced, the abundance of jobs restored confidence that America was still a land of opportunity.

Unfortunately all that began to change in 2001 under the Bush administration. During that period from 2001 to 2009, the American workers experienced what could be the largest job loss in recent U.S. history; and with the country headed for the biggest depression ever recorded, unions in America remained complacent and lethargic.

Chapter 2

Labor Unions' Struggle to Survive

When the economy flourished, many unions did not feel a need to elect the most qualified person to lead their union anymore. This shortsightedness cost the unions dearly during the next decade (2001-2011).

Many unions lost so much during this period of time, they may never fully recover. In order for unions to survive in this climate, union members must get and stay involved, go to meetings, and monitor and ensure that the persons that they selected are indeed doing the job that they were elected to do.

Many union leaders today possess little, if any, labor knowledge mainly because most union officials today are not elected on their ability to serve the local; instead they are elected by friendship or popularity.

When matched with experience negotiators, these individuals fall far short of their adversaries, causing unions to fall farther and farther behind.

Management, on the other hand, is constantly finding new ways to take away many of the gains fought for and won by unions. Here are some of the reasons management have had success against unions over recent years.

In the past, aspiring union stewards would take labor courses *before* running for an elected position. Once elected to an office, labor training became even more intense for the newly elected officers.

Today, that is no longer the case. In most cases, individuals who are elected to office move into that office with little or no training.

Management, with most of their negotiators having twenty-five or more years of experience, waste no time taking advantage of that situation.

Electing a friend with limited labor knowledge to represent union members and their livelihood is like asking a grade school athlete to compete with a professional. It's almost impossible.

The few unions that are successful do elect the most qualified labor individuals available. By doing that, these unions put themselves on the same playing field as management.

It is unfortunate, but most union members have been dumb down to a point where they no longer ask pertinent questions of their leaders, leaving crucial decisions regarding their jobs and livelihoods up to union officers whose main concern today seems to be focused on how much money they can squeeze out of their membership.

Many union members have been kept in the dark and are unaware of what their rights are and, in some cases, what the union movement is all about. In many unions, this is done on purpose.

An inferior union leader fears an educated membership. It is to the inferior leader's personal advantage to keep their members in the dark. By doing so, it gives that union leader an opportunity to remain in office even though he/she may be incompetent. This is true with both local and national union leaders.

Most unions are blessed with smart, intelligent, and forward-thinking men and women; any one of them could be great leaders with dedication and training. Unfortunately most of these individuals are not elected because union members do not take the necessary time to examine the union candidate's qualifications.

COMPLACENCY HAS BECOME A CANCER FOR UNION WORKERS.

Two examples of severe union complacency can be found in the strong union city of Chicago, Illinois, home of Amalgamated Transit Union (ATU) local 241 and ATU local 308. In 2006, a bus driver was elected president of ATU local 241—one of the most powerful local unions in the country.

Unfortunately for those members, the bus driver had little or no labor training. After being elected into office, the driver was taken right off the bus and placed into the office of president/BA.

The same thing happened to the sister local ATU local 308, which represents trainmen. This operator was elected president and had never even filed a grievance before. And now the locals are paying in a big way.

ATU local 241 represents bus operators with a membership that exceeds seven thousand (7,000). In order to have a legal union meeting, local 241 bylaws require that a qualm of one hundred union members must attend that meeting.

For the last several years, local 241 has become so complacent that the local has been unable to conduct the union's business at their local union meeting because they cannot get a qualm of one hundred members from the seven thousand members in their local to attend the once-a-month meetings.

Because they are unable to get a qualm for a meeting, the union officials are allowed (per their bylaws) to make all decisions regarding the local, including distribution of union funds.

Because of the membership's complacency, the union and the company took total advantage of the situation. The union officials began to spend the union funds like drunken sailors.

Some union officials just simply took money out of the union treasury for themselves, some paid their mortgage with membership funds, some union officials even paid for relatives' funerals with union member funds, and others simply used union funds to open personal accounts. Millions of dollars of the members' funds were unaccounted for.

The situation with these elected officials got so out of hand, the International ATU had to come in and take over the local.

The international representatives came in and removed the top official and many others from office. The fate of those officers are pending.

These two locals are now suffering from a barrage of attacks by the company. The downfall of these two locals began when the membership, like so many other union members around the country, became too complacent and stopped electing the most qualified individuals to run their local unions.

This proved to be devastating for these two locals in Illinois and for many other locals around the country that have become ineffective as a result of complacency.

ATU LOCAL 308/241 AT ONE TIME BOASTED SOME OF THE BEST BENEFITS IN THE COUNTRY.

ATU locals 241 and 308 were among the top wage earners in mass transportation. After contract negotiations in 2006, not only did the two locals fall way behind their piers in transportation in wages, but also the way their contract is now constructed, members of local 241 and 308 may never get another wage increase.

According to the new bargaining agreement, the company can go into local 241's and 308's contract and legally remove portions of the members' wages/take-home pay, whenever the company deems it necessary.

The same inexperienced union leaders gave away the local's sacred No Lay-Off Clause. Local 241/308 had a unique no lay-off clause in their contract. Something very few unions had in America. The clause simply read, "If a union worker has two (2) or more years of service with the company, he/she cannot be laid off." This clause had been a part of the contract for more than thirty years.

The clause had to be updated every contract year. Unfortunately during contract negotiations in 2006, the inexperienced union leaders were unaware that the clause had to be updated, therefore giving the company the right to remove the no lay-off clause from their contract; and of course, the company did just that.

The two locals also boasted one of the best pension plans in the country.

Before the election of unqualified union leaders, local 308/241 and the company had equal control of the pension (five trustees for management and five trustees for labor).

With this makeup, it required three votes from labor and three votes from management to move forward on any item regarding the 1.6-billion-dollar pension plan. As soon as the inexperienced individuals were elected into office, they were conned into giving up the union's control of the pension to management.

The new makeup of trustees is now five for labor and six for management, with majority rule. Although union members contribute over 90 percent of the funds that go into the plan, the union no longer has a say in the allocation of the pension funds or the day-to-day operation of the plan.

Management immediately began to dismantle the pension as soon as they took control by taking away many of the benefits that were paid for by members who contributed to the plan for years, expecting to have a livable retirement.

Prior to this contract, retiree health care benefits were paid for by the plan. Management and union workers who were vested in the pension were equally responsible for funding the retiree health care benefits through employee contributions. After the 2006 contract, the company was no longer responsible for funding its share of the retiree's health care.

Management created a Health Care Trust allegedly to fund retiree health care. It requires members of the plan to contribute unlimited contributions to the HCT. The Health Care Trust committee consists of seven trustees—three from labor and four from management, with majority rule.

Even though the company does not make contributions to the health care trust, they put themselves in control of all of the funds in the health care trust. The company decides who will get the millions of dollars from the fund for investments, what law firms will represent the plan, etc.

They also control what personnel will be hired, how much active workers will contribute to the trust fund, and what will be allocated to the retirees. The workers, who contribute all of the funding to the health care trust, have no input.

Some retirees were hit so hard by management's takeover that they are unable to get their life-saving prescriptions. Retirees, whose premiums were previously paid by the plan, are now forced to pay 45 percent of their health care premiums, causing many retirees to lose their homes, life savings, and much more. Management forced active members to quadruple their contribution to the plan.

Management also forced part-time workers to pay into a health care trust for when the part-timer retires. The only problem with that is part-time workers are not vested in the pension plan and can never retire under this plan.

This was all done after the auditor general's report, which showed that as a result of the company not making its proper contributions, the pension became vulnerable.

When questioned about the legality of their actions, the union officials simply claimed that it was not their fault—it was those darn legislators.

Chapter 3

Unions and the Middle Class

Labor unions created the middle class. Corporate and the right wing has been on a mission to destroy the middle-class workers in America for many decades.

In order to accomplish this mission, corporate realizes that they must destroy the labor union movement because it is the labor unions that stand between them and their attempts to dismantle the middle-class workers.

What union members and other middle-class workers should realize is that without labor unions, there would be no middle class; the rich would get richer, and the poor would get poorer.

Without the protection of labor, companies can and will undo many of the gains that unions have bargained and won for workers over the years. Just as they are doing in Chicago.

Corporate understands this and know that without the protection of labor unions, companies could simply eliminate holidays, force workers to work any hours that they desire, discharge workers without just cause, cut or eliminate vacations, destroy pensions, and much, much more.

Previously it was tough for big corporates and the right wing to accomplish some of these goals because of the laws that govern our country. However, corporations are making efforts to change the laws by soliciting politicians, mainly from the right to do their dirty work.

They are also using members of the Supreme Court. Just recently, the Supreme Court, lead by Judge Roberts, ruled that corporations are people. If corporations are people, shouldn't unions be people also? Shouldn't unions be given the right to use union funds to support candidates of their choice just the same as corporates?

Giving corporations the right to buy our legislators is very dangerous. Not only can this destroy the middle-class worker. This could very well endanger our constitution and in fact our country. Any foreign leader with wealth could buy US politicians and use our own constitution against us.

In 2010, the state of Wisconsin elected a right wing republican governor and a right wing republican House and Senate that was hell bent on dismantling labor unions in the state of Wisconsin.

In all fairness to the voters in Wisconsin, none of these politicians campaigned on the fact that they were going to attempt to eliminate unions. Although the signs were there for many years, union leaders were lulled to sleep by corporate lies in regard to the reasons for the state of the economy.

Two weeks after being sworn into office, these same Wisconsin legislators (at the request of big business) placed a bill on the floor that virtually dismantles all public employees' right to bargain in the state of Wisconsin.

These politicians in Wisconsin were bought and paid for by corporate giants like the *Koch* brothers. The governor of Wisconsin, Scott Walker, admitted on tape that his claims that unions were responsible for the alleged problems in the state budget were false. He was caught on film discussing his plan to destroy unions and middle-class workers by dividing the people in the state.

The voters of Wisconsin became fed up with Walker and his cronies and partitioned for a recall of this governor. The people of Wisconsin were tremendously successful with the partition. Voters in Wisconsin collected over a million signatures, more than enough to recall the governor, and was granted a recall.

With the help of the media and corporate money, Walker was able to retain his office. Corporations poured thirty million dollars into the governor's campaign ($30,000,000) while his opponent Milwaukee mayor, Tom Barrette, was only able to raise three million dollars ($3,000,000).

With Walker's dismantling of public unions comes taking away their bargaining rights, pension, wages, health care, and jobs. Forty percent (40%) of union workers voted for Scott Walker in the new election. Was this because of corporate financing Walker, or because unions are still asleep?

This attack on the middle-class worker happened not only in Wisconsin, but also in the majority of the states controlled by republicans around the country. This should never have happened; labor unions should have been ahead of the curve.

Chapter 4

ATTACKS THROUGH THE MEDIA

How CORPORATE AND
THE RIGHT DOMINATE THE SUNDAY TALK SHOWS

Another way corporations and the right have attacked the working class is through the media. The media in America is controlled by many of the same corporations that are hell-bent on destroying the labor movement.

According to a study done in 2005 and 2006, the media has been totally slanted to the right and in the direction of corporates.

By controlling the media, corporation has a large influence on the way people think and act. Corporates have taken full advantage of this situation in their efforts to destroy the middle class.

Every Sunday morning, some of the country's most powerful and influential figures enact one of the most hallowed rituals in American politics: policymakers, government officials, journalists, and other newsmakers appear as guests on the network talk shows to hold forth on the pressing issues of the day.

The shows—ABC's *This Week*, CBS's *Face the Nation*, NBC's *Meet the Press*, and Fox Broadcasting Co.'s *Fox News Sunday*—serve as an invaluable forum for the nation's agenda-setters. It is on these Sunday shows where conventional wisdom is formed and the terms of debate are set.

The study classified every guest appearing on these programs during 2005 and 2006 (over two thousand appearances in all) by their party affiliation and ideology.

The results show that the right has a distinct advantage in determining the shape of the debate on Sunday morning. During the years of the 109th Congress, Republicans and conservatives far outnumbered their Democratic and progressive counterparts on the Sunday morning talk shows.

- Republicans and conservatives dramatically outnumbered Democrats and progressives on the Sunday shows in 2005 and 2006, by a margin of 44 percent to 27 percent (the remainder were neutral or nonpartisan figures).
- Counting only elected officials and administration representatives, Republicans had a stark advantage over Democrats, 62 percent to 37 percent.
- *Fox News Sunday*'s journalist panels are the most lopsided, with a typical lineup consisting of two or even three conservatives, one neutral reporter, and one progressive. But even on ABC, NBC, and CBS, conservative journalists were nearly twice as likely as their progressive counterparts to appear on the Sunday shows.
- While a majority of guest panels on the ABC, NBC, and CBS shows were balanced or neutral in their composition,

there were nearly three times as many right-leaning panels as left-leaning ones. *Fox News Sunday* was even worse.

- The most frequent guests on the Sunday shows during the 2005-2006 study were Sen. Joseph R. Biden Jr. (D-DE), with thirty-eight appearances; Secretary of State Condoleezza Rice, with thirty appearances; and Sen. John McCain (R-AZ), also with thirty appearances.
- And unlike most elected officials, McCain was almost always given a solo interview rather than being paired with a colleague from the opposing party.
- The Sunday shows granted far more solo interviews to Republicans and conservatives than to Democrats and progressives. The top two Republicans to be interviewed solo—Rice and McCain, together—were interviewed solo twice as often as the top two Democrats to be interviewed solo, Biden and Democratic National Committee Chairman Howard Dean.

When the representatives of the three shows were contacted and informed of the results, they all made the same argument in response: Republicans dominated because they were in power.

"One needs to consider that the party holding the presidency also has a cabinet full of major newsmaker guests that speak to U.S. policy matters . . . The same would be true for the eight years of the Clinton administration," said Betsy Fischer, executive producer of *Meet the Press*.

Although their arguments about the Clinton years being the mirror image of the Bush years were simply mistaken, Republicans and conservatives actually had an advantage during the second

Clinton term, which turned into a huge gap once Bush took office; none could explain why conservative journalists so dramatically outnumber progressive journalists on their shows.

This question has absolutely nothing to do with which party controls either end of Pennsylvania Avenue. The imbalance existed on all the Sunday morning shows when Bill Clinton was president and continued throughout the presidency of George W. Bush and Barack Obama.

The realities of power have changed, and Democrats now control the White House and the Senate.

Have we seen a shift in the guest lists on the Sunday shows? [No] Have Democrats been brought on with greater frequency? [No] Have progressive journalists been offered the same opportunity to appear that conservative journalists enjoy? [No] Are the producers of these programs willing to publicly state that they will make an effort to institute such a change? [No]

ALL FOUR SUNDAY SHOWS LEAN RIGHT

Throughout the years of the 109th Congress, the four Sunday shows displayed a troublesome pattern: Republicans and conservatives outnumbered Democrats and progressives in every category, on every program, across the board.

Few will be surprised to learn that *Fox News Sunday* was the most conservative-leaning of the shows. Among the three other network shows, *Face the Nation* was the worst offender in 2005 and 2006, giving Republicans and conservatives a 15-point edge over Democrats and progressives.

Meet the Press and *This Week* gave Republicans and conservatives a 10-point and 11-point advantage over Democrats and progressives, respectively.

The discussions held on the shows frequently determine the scope of official debate in Washington, legitimizing some views and—by nature of their absence—marginalizing others.

The voice of the middle-class worker is not being heard. Take a look at the charts below, and you will see how one-sided the media has become over the last few decades.

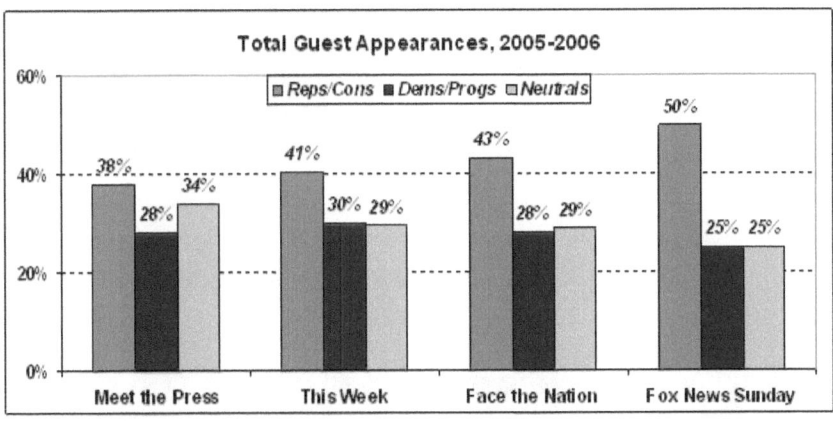

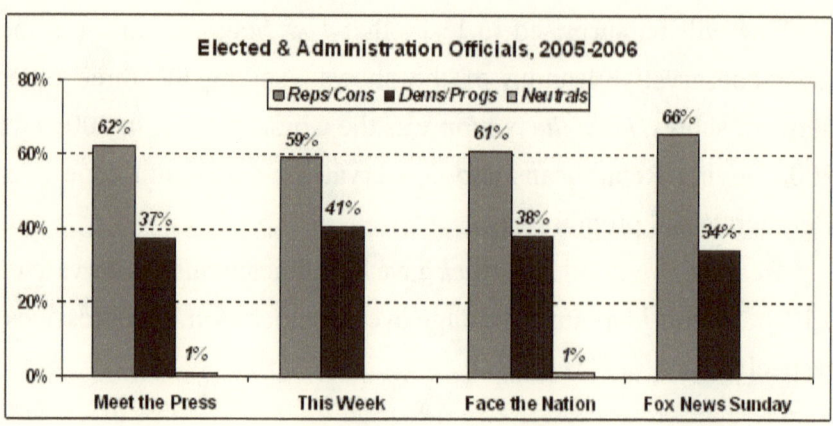

Elected & Administration Officials, 2005-2006

Reps/Cons · Dems/Progs · Neutrals

	Meet the Press	This Week	Face the Nation	Fox News Sunday
Reps/Cons	62%	59%	61%	66%
Dems/Progs	37%	41%	38%	34%
Neutrals	1%		1%	

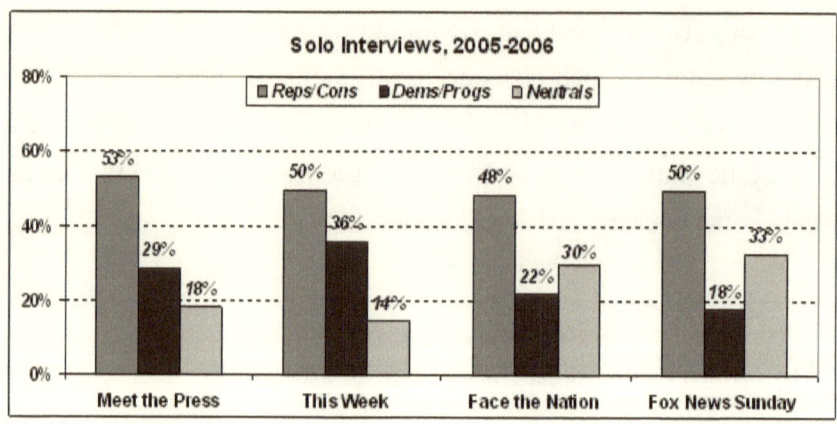

Solo Interviews, 2005-2006

Reps/Cons · Dems/Progs · Neutrals

	Meet the Press	This Week	Face the Nation	Fox News Sunday
Reps/Cons	53%	50%	48%	50%
Dems/Progs	29%	36%	22%	18%
Neutrals	18%	14%	30%	33%

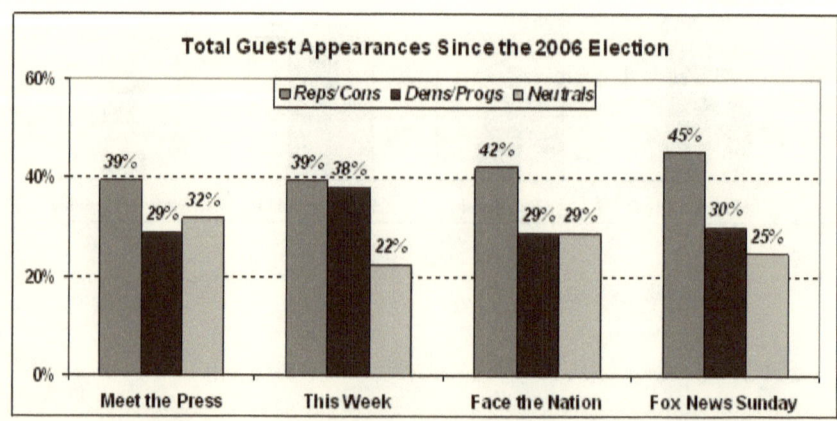

Total Guest Appearances Since the 2006 Election

Reps/Cons · Dems/Progs · Neutrals

	Meet the Press	This Week	Face the Nation	Fox News Sunday
Reps/Cons	39%	39%	42%	45%
Dems/Progs	29%	38%	29%	30%
Neutrals	32%	22%	29%	25%

Chapter 5

Why Does Corporate America Fear Negotiating with Labor Unions?

After all, negotiating is where the two parties sit down and discuss work-related issues and possible solutions. Unions cannot force companies to do anything that the company decides it does not want to do.

Unlike a general business negotiation and lawsuit negotiations that are not regulated by statutory provisions, a collective bargaining negotiation is mandated and governed by external laws that make it *fair* for both sides.

Many different statutes come into play during the negotiation process. Private sector bargaining encounters are regulated by the National Labor Relations Act (NLRA) for most workers and by the Railway Labor Act (RLA) for railroad and airline personnel.

Federal workers are covered by the Civil Service Reform Act, while state and local government personnel are under state public sector bargaining laws.

Labor unions have the right to demand bargaining over the wages, hours, and working conditions of the affected employees. On the other hand, the NLRA specifically indicates that the duty to bargain does not require either party to agree to specific proposals or to make concessions.

They are merely obliged to meet at regular times and to discuss the pertinent issues in good faith. One aspect of labor-management negotiations that is different from many other types of bargaining interactions involves the ongoing relationship between the parties.

After collective discussions are completed, the parties must continue to deal with each other. Union and management negotiators must continue to meet to resolve disagreements that may occur with respect to the application of bargaining agreement provisions, and employees and managers must work together to produce profitable goods or services if the firm is to be successful.

If union negotiators drive a hard bargain that unduly inflates labor costs, management can flat out refuse to agree. So why do corporates want to prevent unions from having the right to bargain? It's the word "GREED"; corporate would like to have little or no resistance to their demands.

A factor which makes collective bargaining interactions relatively unique entails the many issues that have to be addressed. Many types of compensation have to be discussed, including hourly wages, piecework rates, fringe benefits such as pensions and health care and similar issues. What hours will the employees have to work, when will breaks and meal periods be scheduled? Unfortunately big corporations have demonstrated their desire to take workers back to the days when horses were considered more valuable than humans at the workplace.

There will always be distributive items that both sides value. These issues generally entail monetary terms. Even in this area, however, if negotiators are willing to think outside the box and seek innovative solutions, they may be able to expand the pie and simultaneously enhance their respective positions.

The problem with this approach is that large corporations somehow believe that they are entitled to the whole pie. For example, having their legislative friends pass laws that prohibit collective bargaining.

Negotiating parties occasionally encounter difficult topics that neither side can surrender without a substantial loss of face. If they are unable to obtain a mutually acceptable outcome, they can invoke the contractual grievance-arbitration procedures and ask an outside neutral to decide the matter.

As noted earlier, the duty to bargain does not require that either party agree to any particular demands or the making of concessions. If after thorough bargaining, the parties have reached presently irreconcilable positions, either party can demand that the final proposal be placed before the membership for a vote or opt for arbitration.

GLOBALIZATION

GLOBALIZATION'S EFFECT ON AMERICA'S MIDDLE CLASS

The world we live in today is one of global proportions. Gone are the days where retail stores were filled with products that were "made in America."

Today we are more likely to find products made in China, Taiwan, Bangladesh, or Mexico. But what does this mean to Americans? How does this shift in our nation's economy affect the average American? How does this shift affect our middle class?

The answers to these questions are not simple. Advances in technology have quickly brought our nation into a fast-moving worldwide market. While many would agree that these technological advances are good for humanity as a whole, I would argue that this rapid advancement to globalizing societies comes with some very steep costs.

While there are still many manufacturing jobs owned by American corporations, you will not find them in the U.S. The one percent moved the jobs from America to countries with cheap labor.

In *The World Is Flat* by Thomas L. Friedman, a *New York Times* columnist, Friedman goes through the timeline of technological development, mainly in the communications arena, and the effects this rapid advancement has had on America, in particular.

What Friedman comes to realize is that the technology that has rapidly catapulted our nation into the global market has also had a negative impact on our society.

What does he mean by this? The same advances that allow us to communicate and access the rest of the world also makes our markets open to them.

The fact that these lines of communication are now open allows these other nations to get in the game, so to speak, providing direct competition to American workers.

This easy access to cheap labor has had a direct impact on American jobs, due to corporate outsourcing, which prior to globalization was never a concern. In effect, globalization by big corporations has made America very vulnerable in this arena.

So how does this affect us?

There are various opinions which place all the blame on outsourcing for our "disappearing middle class." In *Global Outsourcing and the Disappearing Middle Class* by William Raynor of the State University of New York, Raynor specifically discusses the impact outsourcing has had on our economy and the middle class here in the U.S.

Not all of the job losses here in America can be attributed to outsourcing, but it has had a significant, negative impact on our economy. Ready access to cheap, uneducated workers essentially puts many American jobs on the line.

So is it true that the hardest hit is the middle class in this loss of jobs? Absolutely! The drop in the number of workers hired by American employers as well as the quality of those jobs are devastating to the American family.

Only a few of the 116,000 private sector jobs created recently provide good incomes . . . the remainder consist of temps, retail trade, telephone marketing, etc. A decline such as this in the quality of these jobs has a huge impact on employees' ability to survive financially. This, in turn, impacts our entire economy.

Interestingly enough, there are many who believe the "middle class" that we have accepted as the norm for generations really is an anomaly. While it's true that there has been a shift in wealth over the last three or four decades, the gap between rich and poor is growing, and the middle class appears to be losing ground.

Prior to the Depression, there were the rich and the poor or the struggling. As the rich get richer, they attain more power. Those with power make public policy (or influence those that do).

Therefore, those policies that are created will be created with the most powerful (wealthiest) in mind. In effect, the cycle builds upon itself, creating its own cocoon of self-protection. In effect, one percent is trying to take America back to the glory days of the wealthy, where there were only rich and poor.

Policies that are designed to protect one segment of society come with a cost to those it is not designed to protect. In this case, policies that are designed to favor the wealthiest American taxpayers, in effect, hurt the rest of the taxpayers by passing along higher tax rates, broader tax policies, making less funding available for service providers, etc.

As there is a limit to the "pie," if one large piece goes to one segment of society, the rest must get smaller pieces.

The majority of countries in the world (e.g., Mexico) have two classes: the ruler who are very, very rich and the rest of the people who are very, very poor. America is different, because we built our society with the belief that anyone can live the "American Dream" and prosper if one works hard.

Globalization is hurting the U.S. by providing cheap products and labor from other nations who "don't play by the rules." The overall sentiment is that "the effects of globalization are not equal."

While globalization is a boon to Asia and India, wages for many American workers are down substantially or have remained the same over the last five years. This direct competition with substantially cheaper labor and goods has had a direct negative impact on working Americans' ability to provide for their families.

United States has lost more than three million jobs since the Bush administration took office. The fact is America cannot compete with cheap labor from Asia and India. The fact that these workers do not have access to the same benefits as American workers makes the cost even less for companies looking to outsource. And this is an alarming trend.

The loss of these neighborhoods is a clear indication of this economic class as a whole. Middle-class neighborhoods are shrinking at more than twice the rate of the middle class itself. In their place, poor and rich neighborhoods are both on the rise. The decline is a result of widening income inequality in our nation.

This economic inequality is perpetuated by policymakers who seek to protect their wealth and power. Much of our nation's wealth is held now by CEOs who earn their wealth by taking advantage of cheap goods and labor, namely, globalization.

Deregulation in the '70s and '80s opened up a whole new global market. It was just a matter of time before corporations around the world, American companies included, began to take advantage of this cheap labor market.

In the U.S., the average wage for a computer programmer is up to $80,000 per year. In India, a programmer can expect to average just $11,000 per year. The instant savings for corporations are not generally passed on to the consumer. Instead, corporate profits explode, and top-heavy administrations receive excessive salaries and benefits. Ultimately, it is the average worker that suffers.

One needs only to look around to see the downturn in the U.S. economy. Rising interest rates, layoffs, cutbacks, reductions in or elimination of pensions, lost jobs, rising consumer debt, reduced housing starts, the rising cost of education . . . the average "middle-class" American is finding it increasingly difficult to make ends meet.

These economic factors impact families negatively, despite working hard; many families are finding that their standard of living has dropped. And it's unlikely to improve any time soon.

Those living currently in the "middle class" are usually just one illness, layoff, or divorce away from poverty. Yet presented with these same crises, the rich do not suffer the same devastation as the middle class. Our policymakers need to take a long, hard look at the real long-term "costs" to America that are associated with these short-term savings.

Because of unions and the middle class, America is the most powerful country in the world. If we allow corporate to destroy the middle class, America can very well become another third world country.

Chapter 6

CAN LABOR UNIONS MAKE A COMEBACK?

With all of these odds stacked against it, reversing the downward trend of labor will not be an easy task. Labor unions will first have to reestablish themselves as leaders and creators of the middle class. Labor unions need to recognize the union's short falls.

Electing inefficient, incompetent union leaders pushes labor and the middle class farther and farther behind big corporations who are destroying not only the middle class but America itself.

Many unions have lost their identity and are unions in name only. Some unions lack the training and knowledge needed to fight the corporate takeovers.

Labor unions and the middle class need to understand that the real power is in the people.

If unions are going to prevail, they will have to educate and mobilize people in every neighborhood in America.

In cases where local unions fall short on educating its members, the middle class, others in the labor movement, and international unions will have to pick up the slack.

Labor unions and the working middle class should always partner with elected officials in their state, town, etc., and most importantly, partner with the community in areas that affect the middle class.

Unions and middle-class workers must also work continuously to assure that anyone elected in their state or town is pro labor and pro middle class.

If union members really want to strengthen a weak union, the union member should understand what his/her responsibilities are.

- It is the responsibility of the national and local unions to see that their representatives are properly trained.
- It is the responsibility of the membership to examine the candidate's qualifications before voting that person into office.

If these changes are not made, unions will continue to dwindle. If the middle-class worker and unions ever expect to move back to the center, unions and middle-class workers are going to have to go back to what has worked for them in the past—*choosing smart, dedicated leaders.*

If labor unions continue to allow their members to be dumb down by nonproductive union officers, by the media, and by legislators bought and paid for *by big corporations, this trend will continue; and unions along with the middle class* will *disappear.*

Because of our democracy, America is the greatest country in the world. We did not become the greatest country in the world because of big corporations. America became great because of the middle-class worker and labor unions.

Large corporations are not generally concerned about the working class here in America. Greed seems to be their only driving force. Can labor unions make a comeback? In a word yes, will they?

That will be left entirely up to the unions and the middle class. So long as union members are in this period of ungratefulness, complacency, and ignorance, unions will continue to digress.

Chapter 7

THE NEGOTIATOR AND
A MODEL UNION LEADER

BY RONALD ROACH

*My name is Ronald Roach. I've worked for and have done research on labor leaders for many years. One of the people that I researched happens to be the author of this book, **Mr. Jerry W. Williams Sr.***

I met Mr. Williams through a mutual acquaintance in the midseventies, and I've been following his career ever since. This chapter can be a book in itself.

Williams, who comes from a union background, is a former union steward for the United Auto Workers of America (ATU) and a former representative for the Brotherhood of Radio Workers of America. He was appointed union steward for the Amalgamated Transit Union in 1979.

Like many other union stewards during those times, Williams took labor classes and earned labor degrees at institutions such as Roosevelt University, the George Meany Institute, etc. He was elected to the executive board position at ATU local 308 and was required to take additional extensive labor courses at other universities.

After a successful stint as an executive board member, Williams was elected president/business agent for the local in 1993. The international ATU put Williams and other local ATU presidents through even more extensive training and required additional labor studies at the University of Illinois, labor institutions in Minnesota, Washington DC, and Canada, where they earned several degrees in labor.

Armed with that labor knowledge and background, one of Williams's first moves as president was to reach out and embrace the community and community organizations. I personally recall a meeting he had with some of the community groups in Chicago where some of the leaders spoke up and commended Williams for his involvement with the community.

One community leader stated that her group had long wanted to work with the labor unions but was unable to get labor to respond on any major issues, especially transportation.

Williams reassured the groups at that meeting that the lack of cooperation with the transit workers union in regard to the community would end under his watch. He told the group that "you are why we exist."

As soon as he was elected president, Williams moved to form an alliance with the Illinois legislators and lawmakers. He was tremendously successful with both Democrats and Republicans.

Williams called for a forum with the community and Illinois legislators at the Thompson Center in downtown Chicago. The forum drew a tremendous response from top union officials in Illinois, several community organizations, and both state and local elected officials.

At the breakout sessions, local leaders, community organizations, and legislators formed committees to discuss the plight of mass transportation in the state.

These committees addressed the problem and possible solutions to the lack of funding for mass transit in the state. After several meetings with legislators and community organizations such as Citizen Action of Illinois, Metro Seniors in Action, Citizens Taking Action, and many more; the stage was set to move forward.

President Williams hired a labor research firm headed by Ken Blum and Robert Ginsburg, Ph. D. "The Midwest Center for Labor Research" is to do a study of funding for mass transportation in state of Illinois.

The project was called Build Illinois. Once the project was developed, President Williams of Amalgamated Transit Union local 308 and presidents from other transit locals such as ATU local 241, ATU, local 1028, UTU Metra, and other project participants campaigned all over the state for the Build Illinois *transit project, appearing on local radio and TV programs around the state, pointing out the roll of mass transit in the state of Illinois.*

This group was able to demonstrate to the people of Illinois the need for increased funding for the transit systems in the state.

After getting solid support from the people in the state, Williams was able to cross the aisle in Springfield and get support from both Democrat and Republican legislators with the help of a young state senator. By the name of Barack Obama.

The Build Illinois *project was presented to the governor of Illinois, and with a few changes the Build Illinois project was renamed and became the* Illinois First *program.*

Because of his ability to forge good relationships with legislators and community organizations, the governor from Illinois asked Williams if he would be willing to work on the governor's Illinois First *committee.*

The committee's responsibility was to find new revenue in the state to help finance schools, assisted living, transportation, etc.

The committee identified and secured 12.1 billion dollars in new state revenue for the affected agencies. Thanks to Williams, 4.1 billion dollars was allocated for transportation in the state of Illinois, and 2.1 of the 4.1 billion allocated for transportation went to the city of Chicago for the Chicago Transit Authority.

The highlight of the Illinois First *program was that it went a long way in helping to resolve the budget crisis in the state. The community, the legislators, and the unions were all satisfied with the results. Williams went on to help launch the careers of several legislators that attended that forum including Congresswoman Jan Schakowski, state Sen. Willie Delgado, and many more.*

THE NEGOTIATOR

Jerry Williams Sr. was elected and reelected three times as president of ATU local 308. During that period of time, the local experienced more improvements than at any other time in the local's history.

President Williams negotiated the highest pay increase in the history of the local—$1.66 per hour in 1996 and an additional $3.00 *per hour pay increase in 2001. Prior to the Williams administration, the highest negotiated pay increase for 241/308 workers was 82¢ per hour. This was negotiated back in the mideighties.*

The two increases under Williams increased members' take-home pay by $9,692 per year for each union member. During his tenure as president at ATU local 308, Jerry Williams negotiated over a total of thirty million dollars ($30,000,000) in wage increases for his local union membership.

[Members who retired under President Williams's administration received, on average, $7,000 more per year in benefits which amounts to additional $600 per month.]

When the company pushed to eliminate the ticket agent, President Williams not only saved the ticket agent's job by negotiating an agreement to allow the agents to become customer assistants but also negotiated a $2.00 an hour pay increase for the agents in the middle of a contract year.

By Ronald Roach

Research Engineer Ronald Roach

September 9, 1999

Jerry Williams, Sr.
President
Amalgamated Transit Union - Local 308
205 West Wacker Drive
#700
Chicago, IL 60606

Dear Jerry:

As a token of our appreciation for your help on the Illinois First Task Force, please accept this engraved pen commemorating your invaluable assistance in what is, by all accounts, one of the most successful task force efforts of any type in Illinois history.

Citizens in every county of this state will benefit for years to come from your efforts. Participation by individuals like you on civic efforts such as this never get enough recognition, but I want you to know how much I appreciate all your work.

Sincerely,

George H. Ryan
Governor

President Williams conducts huge voter drive

President Williams and House Speaker Michael Madigan

PRESIDENT HOLDS A FORUM TO FUND MASS TRANSPORTATION AT THE THOMPSON CENTER IN CHICAGO, ILLINOIS.

State Sen. Willie Delgado

Chicago alderman, Joe Moore

President Williams

Chicago Federation of Labor president Don Turner

Jackie Leavey, president of the Neighborhood Budget Capital Group
(NBCG)

Congresswoman Jan Schakowsky

President Williams/Illinois attorney general, Lisa Madigan

President Williams and Illinois Governor Rod Blagojevich

Former local 241 president Isaiah Thomas, CTA chairman Valarie Jarrett (presently chief advisor to President Barack Obama), CTA president F. Karusi and former local 308 president Jerry Williams Sr.

Former local 241 president Isaiah Thomas,former local 308 president Jerry Williams Sr.,CTA chairman Valarie Jarrett (presently chief advisor to President Barack Obama) and CTA president F. Karusi

Karusi, Congressman Bobby Rush, Thomas, Williams

County Clerk David Orr and President Williams

New York congressman Charles Rangel and President Williams

Vice President Al Gore and President Williams who was an
Al Gore delegate in 2000 election.

www.ingramcontent.com/pod-product-compliance
Lightning Source LLC
Chambersburg PA
CBHW050338290526
45785CB00006B/2547